Because of the many skills and industries involved in the making of any book, the cooperation and assistance of numerous people were necessary to produce this particular one. The author and publisher wish to extend their thanks to the following: Claude G. Williams, Miss Stephanie Valky, Harvey M. Soldan and Jack D. Vail of Vail-Ballou Press, Inc.; F. Stewart Crosley and Robert W. Schwab of Kingsport Press, Inc.; Peter Markovich of Capper Engraving Company, Inc.; Edward B. Rae and Robert S. Van Dyke of Rae Lithographers; Bernard Kaye and Jack Schwartz of Sterling-Regal Engraving Company, Inc.; and Rus Anderson.

HOW BOOKS ARE MADE

DODD, MEAD & COMPANY · NEW YORK   BY DAVID C. COOKE

In the world of publishing there is no one of
greater importance to an author than his editor,
and I respectfully dedicate this book to mine,

S. Phelps Platt, Jr.

without whose untiring effort over many months,
this work could not have been published in its
present form.

Frontispiece photo courtesy of Kingsport Press, Inc.

CONTENTS

THE BEGINNING OF A BOOK

A book begins with an idea. That idea when developed, worked over, and put down on paper by an author becomes a manuscript. It may be on one of many subjects—a story, a play, a history, about nature, mathematics or even how books are made. The manuscript is then submitted to a company—the book publisher—whose staff determines whether it is worthy of being made into printed books. Many, many manuscripts are sent to book publishers daily, but very few are accepted for publication. For books are costly to produce; the publisher can afford to invest only in those manuscripts that make good reading, are well written, fill a definite need on a subject, and therefore will be used by thousands of people.

Many people in a publisher's office have a say in the acceptance of a manuscript. The editors must decide if it is well written, if it is interesting, and whether there are other books similar to it. The sales department asks, Can we sell this as a book to stores, libraries, and dealers? The production staff determines if the manuscript can be made into a book for a price that will appeal to buyers. The advertising and promotion departments give their opinions.

Once a book-publishing house has accepted the manuscript and has made an agreement, or contract, with the author as to his payment, editing begins. Editing can mean hours of work by an editor, who may suggest that parts of the manuscript be rewritten or that new material be added. Editing can also mean checking the spelling and punctuation, and looking into reference books to make sure facts and figures are correct.

There comes a time when the manuscript has been thoroughly edited, necessary illustrations have been obtained, and the making of the book begins.

The author and the editor of the book you are reading check the manuscript and select photographs.

THE BOOK IS DESIGNED

The production or manufacturing department of a book-publishing company has the job of supervising the making of books from the edited manuscript.

The first step in producing a book is to decide how the finished volume will look. These are a few of the questions which must be answered: What size will the book be? How many pages will it have? On what kind of paper will the book be printed? What sort of jacket or dust cover will it have? What kind of cloth will there be on the cover of the book? How many copies will be printed?

When each detail has been decided, a careful estimate of all the costs is made and a price for which the book will be sold is determined.

Next, the manuscript with all production details or specifications is turned over to a book designer. This designer decides what kind and size of type will be used. The type selected may be LARGE or small; it may be a wide line of words such as on this page or

a narrow line for a smaller page.

It may be one of many different kinds of types, each of which has a definite name, such as

Baskerville	Caledonia	News Gothic
Bodoni Bold	Caslon	Spartan Medium
Bookman	Janson	Times Roman

and each of which has a little different look. The designer determines how wide the margins will be, the number of lines to a page, where the page numbers are to be located, how the title page will look, and many other details.

The designer draws up a typical page and specifies type to be used.

When the designer has finished his work, the manuscript with complete instructions is sent away by the manager of the book publisher's production department to be set into type. Almost all book publishers have their books made by companies that are expert in printing and binding books. There are many such manufacturers throughout the United States.

SOME TYPE IS SET BY MACHINE

One of man's greatest achievements was the development of movable type, the process by which letters of the alphabet were "set" or put on the edges of pieces of metal. In turn these were covered with ink, a sheet of paper was placed over the type and pressed against it, and when it was pulled away the words remained on the paper. This process is the basis of all printing today.

There was a time when the only books available were those painstakingly written by hand. Then back in the fifteenth century, when movable type was first used to print books, each letter of a word was hand picked from a tray of letters, carefully placed side by side until one line was formed, and line after line arranged to make a page of type. This was a slow, laborious way to set type. Today type is set almost entirely by machines, one of which is called a Linotype.

The Linotype machine is operated something like a typewriter, except that it has many more keys and does not make use of an inked ribbon. When the operator, or "compositor," touches one of the keys on the Linotype machine, a small piece of metal with a letter stamped into it (a "matrix") drops down a chute to a space on the front of the machine. This space is exactly the same length as a line of type in the book will be.

After the compositor has punched out enough words to fill a line, he presses a lever which lifts the entire line of words to a pot of metal that has been heated to a liquid. The spaces between words are automatically made wider, if necessary, so that all lines of type are exactly the same length. Just the right amount of metal is forced out of the pot against the line, and after a few seconds the metal hardens into a bar, or "slug," of type and drops to a tray by the Linotype operator's side. The average person would have trouble trying to read a slug of type from a Linotype machine, since all of the letters and words are backwards. To see what it looks like, hold this book to a mirror and try to read it. Compositors can read these backward slugs as easily as most people can read a printed line.

(Left) An operator at a Linotype machine. Note tray at his side holding lines of type. (Below) A section of a composing room. The piles of lead bars on the floor will be melted in the machines to become type "slugs."

OTHER TYPESETTING METHODS

For some books the production supervisor in the publishing company may decide to use typesetting methods which are entirely different from the Linotype system. If the book is to contain many numbers, symbols, and unusual letters, the compositor is instructed to set the type by a method called "monotype."

Monotype setting consists of two separate machines, a composing machine and a casting machine. The composing machine has a keyboard very much like that on the Linotype, but instead of setting the type, coded marks are punched into a strip of paper. Each letter of the alphabet, each number, each punctuation mark, each symbol appears on the paper strip as a differently shaped hole.

After the coded paper strip emerges from the monotype composing machine, it is fed into the casting machine, which casts on a separate piece of metal each letter or symbol. When type is set by monotype, a compositor may correct errors merely by taking out the wrong letter and substituting the right one, whereas in the Linotype system an entire line must be reset to correct even one misplaced comma.

Another typesetting method is known as "photographic typesetting," or "cold composition," since no hot metal is used. In photographic typesetting when the compositor punches a letter or a number on his keyboard, a tiny photograph is made of that letter. The result is a film negative, just as the click of a camera exposes the picture taken on a negative. Generally, photo-typesetting is used for printing by the photo-offset process, which will be described later in this book.

(Left) The keyboard of a monotype machine. Each key pressed punches a symbol into the tape seen at the top of picture. This tape is then fed into a casting machine which produces letters and words shown in the right photo.

SOME TYPE IS SET BY HAND

Even though today most type is set on automatic machines, some is still set by hand. Hand-set type is usually large in size, and is used where few letters are needed. Such large type is called "display type," and appears in a book on such pages as the title page.

In the composition or setting of type small letters are called "lower case" and capital letters "upper case." Years ago, before typesetting machines were invented, when all type was set by hand, the frequently-used lower-case letters were kept in a tray or "case" on a lower level and therefore were easier to reach than the capital letters, which were higher in the case. Printers no longer use the same kind of type trays that they used in the past, the pieces of type now being kept in sliding drawers. Hand-set type is placed, letter by letter, in a small metal frame called a "stick," which the compositor holds in his hand as he works. One edge of the stick can be moved back and forth to lengthen or shorten the line, and when adjusted, the space is the exact length of the line to be set.

Those working with type use measuring units called "points," "picas," "ems," and "ens." A point is very small, there being 72 points in one inch. A pica is larger, six of them to one inch and each therefore containing 12 points. The size of type is measured by points. You are reading 12-point type, which means that the height of the letters is 12 points. (Six-point type looks like this.) The width of lines is measured in picas. A full line of the type you are reading is 36 picas. White space between words is measured by ems or units of ems. An em originally was the width of a capital M of the size type being measured; half an em is an en. Space between lines is measured by points. There are four points of space between each two lines or slugs of type on this page.

In setting type by hand the compositor inserts letters and spaces into a "stick," set to the width of line desired.

Courtesy of Kingsport Press, Inc.

PROOFS ARE PULLED

As the type comes from a Linotype machine, the metal slugs are transferred to long metal trays or "galleys."

After the slugs in a galley have been inspected and cleaned, the edge of the tray is marked with the job number and galley number, and placed in a storage rack. Type setting for big books may require several weeks, and an accurate record must be kept of all the galleys. A printing plant usually works on many different books at the same time. If a galley for one book is mislaid, or if the tray is marked incorrectly, it would

Below are trays or "galleys" of metal Linotype slugs. Each line of type is a single piece of metal.

A long proof of each galley is made on a proofing press.

be a difficult problem to put it into the correct book at the correct place.

After the type has been set for a book, the galleys are taken from the storage racks, a layer of ink rolled over them, a long strip of paper laid on top, and pressure applied to the paper so that the type is very roughly printed on the sheet. These sheets, so printed one at a time, are called "galley proofs." A single galley usually contains enough type to make three pages in the finished book. Enough proofs are made so that all those who are interested in the book may read them—the author, the editor and others who may want to check the material before it is printed in book form.

GALLEY PROOFS ARE READ

After proofs have been made of the galleys, one set is sent to the composing room's proofreading department. The people who work in this section are experts in finding errors in galley proofs, such as misspelled words, broken letters, crooked lines, and misplaced commas. All errors are marked for correction on a set of galley proofs, and many questions are raised. This becomes the "marked set" of galleys.

Galley proofs are then sent to the publishing company. Here they are checked in the production department; they are sent to the author for checking; the editors read them; some sets may be sent to interested critics.

When everyone has checked them, back go the proofs to the composing room, where all lines containing errors are reset. If one comma has been added, the entire line must be reset, for—remember—in Linotype composition each line of type is one piece or slug of metal.

After all corrections have been made, the galleys of type are divided into pages. The production supervisor in the publisher's office has previously told the compositor what size the pages of the book are to be and how many lines should be on each page. The "makeup man" measures the correct amount of type for each page and adds to it a slug with the page number (called "folio") on it. Some books have "running heads" at the top of each page, usually with the book title on all left-hand pages and the chapter title on the facing pages. These are also added by the makeup man.

Galley proofs are carefully checked for errors. The proof reader on the left reads aloud from the manuscript to her companion who follows on the proof.

Courtesy of Vail-Ballou Press, Inc.

PAGE PROOFS ARE CHECKED

When the type in the galleys has been broken into pages, once again proofs are "pulled" and such proofs are read for errors in the proof room, by the publisher, and often by the author. At this stage it is necessary to insert special page references and to check any footnotes.[*]

It is also necessary to make certain that those illustrations to appear with the type are correctly located. In addition, "front matter" is carefully checked. Front matter is the material that precedes the first chapter of the book and includes the title page, copyright page, acknowledgments, contents page, and others. Especially important is the copyright page, indicating the year in which the book was registered for copyright and in whose name the book is copyrighted. Such a right is obtained by registering the book with the Register of Copyrights in Washington, D.C. The publishing right to a book so registered is thereby established for a specified number of years.

If the book is to have an index, a set of page proofs is turned over to an indexer who makes up the desired listings with proper page references. The index, glossary, and other material that follows the last chapter of a book are called "back matter."

Page proofs are returned to the composing room where all changes and corrections are reset and inserted into their proper places.

[*]This is a footnote. The type for such notes is smaller than the body of the book, in this case being 9-point. Footnotes generally are used to enlarge upon information supplied in the text or to indicate where the author obtained his information.

After corrections have been made, galleys are divided into pages. Proofs are made of these pages and again checked for errors.

Courtesy of Vail-Ballou Press, Inc.

LINE DRAWINGS ARE ENGRAVED

While the words of the book are being set into type, the production department of the publishing company is busy with other matters concerning that book. Many books have illustrations. Some may have drawings, others photographs. If the book is to be illustrated by drawings made especially for it, the publisher's production staff must work closely with an artist. The artist selected is advised as to what kind of paper or material on which his art work is to be drawn, and the best kind of pencil or pen or brush with which to make his drawings.

When the artist has finished, his drawings may be sent to a company called a "photo-engraver." It is the job of the photo-engraver to make a metal plate on which the drawing will appear in relief. If the art work is a simple black-and-white drawing, the photo-engraver makes his plate by first taking a photograph of this illustration with a special camera. He will then have produced a film negative, which he places over a thin sheet of zinc or copper that has been coated with a special chemical. Next, the photo-engraver puts the metal plate and negative under a strong light, which transfers the drawing image in the negative onto the thin metal plate. Finally, the plate is placed in a bath of acid, which eats away the white areas of the picture and leaves the dark areas. The plate is then washed and inspected. A proof of the plate is pulled. When the proof has been approved by the publisher, the plate is ready to join the type of the book.

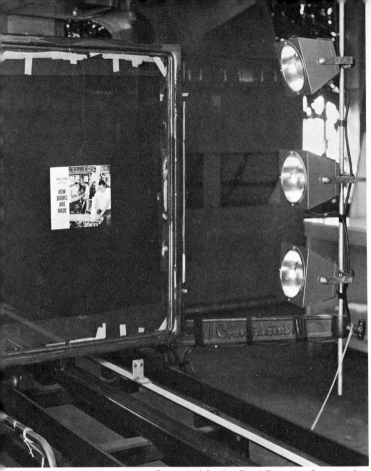

The artwork or picture to be engraved is first placed behind glass in a frame onto which strong lights are flashed.

A large camera, extending from a darkroom, takes a picture of the subject within the frame.

HALFTONES ARE ENGRAVED

To make a printing plate of a photograph, or of a drawing with various shades and lights in it, requires a little different method. Look at a light area of the photograph below under a magnifying glass. You will see that it consists of thousands of tiny dots. The darker the printing, the larger the black dots will be. By these dots, photographs that have not only pure white areas and solid black areas but all variations of grays can be printed on paper.

Courtesy of Sterling-Regal Engraving Company, Inc.

The photo-engraver at left is holding a glass "screen," consisting of thousands of dots. This screen is inserted into the camera when various shades or tones of the picture are to be reproduced.

The exposed film of the camera is carefully developed and inspected.

Courtesy of Sterling-Regal Engraving Company, Inc.

The finished film negative is then used to etch onto a thin sheet of metal the image photographed. The engraver above is developing the metal plate.

The same photo-engraver who made the black-and-white plate described on page 22 photographs the picture or drawing, but between his camera and the picture he puts a glass plate with thousands of dots on it. This glass plate is called a "screen" because it looks like a window screen, only much finer. Some screens have 150 dots per inch and are thus called 150-line screens. Light is flashed on the art work, and the photo-engraver's camera snaps a picture. As the light is reflected from the picture onto the camera negative, it passes through the screen. The white parts of the picture being photographed flash through the screen brightly and take a small part of the dots with them onto the film negative. The dark areas, being not so bright, put almost all of the dots onto the film negative. The result is a negative packed with dots of all sizes. The negative is made into a plate, called a "halftone," just as described in making a line engraving.

It is easy to see why the line engraving will print. Ink, when rolled on the plate, stays on the ridges and will transfer to paper pressed against the plate. Ink rolled onto a halftone plate covers the dots only and again will be transferred to paper.

PRINTING PLATES ARE MADE

Some books are printed right from the slugs of type that have come from the type-setting machine and from the plates made by the photo-engraver. However, the metal in these slugs and in the engravings is too soft to print more than a few thousand copies before it begins to show signs of wear. If many books are to be printed, or if the book is expected to be reprinted frequently, it is necessary to make long-lasting printing plates of the type and the engravings. Such plates are lighter, easier to handle, and more readily stored than type.

A mold has just been made by squeezing soft papier-mâché under heat tightly against the slugs of type that had previously been divided into pages.

Courtesy of Vail-Ballou Press, Inc.

Molten metal, poured onto the mold and let harden, emerges as printing plates, called "stereotypes," when made by this method.

There are many kinds of printing plates. The type of plate selected to be made will depend on what is to be printed, the kind of press to be used, the number of copies to be printed, and other considerations.

If the production department of the book-publishing company has decided to print a book by the "contact" or "letterpress" method, the plates may be made of copper and lead, plastic, rubber, magnesium, or other metals. The process of making plates from type will vary from material to material, but basically it consists of making a mold of each page, such molds being formed by pressing a soft substance like wax or liquid plastic or papier-mâché against the page of type. The mold is removed and liquid metal or plastic or rubber is pressed into it, let harden, and then cleaned as

The metal plates are separated, carefully trimmed and inspected.

A closeup of a printing plate, shown at right locked with others for a special printing.

well as machined to make the edges perfectly straight. Generally such plates are about ⅛ inch thick. All type and pictures for a single page are on one plate. At this point proofs are again pulled, this time of the plates, and these "plate proofs" are carefully checked. This is the last proofing the book will have before being printed.

When the finished plates are all ready, they are transferred into the press room.

Courtesy of Kingsport Press, Inc.

LETTERPRESS PRINTING

Presses for which plates just described are made are of many sizes and shapes and kinds. The simplest is the small hand press you once got for Christmas, which printed calling cards. The most complex is as large as a locomotive and prints on a broad ribbon of paper as wide as a sidewalk.

In general, books are printed on presses that will print a sheet the size of a table-cloth, approximately six feet wide and four feet deep. For the average book, this means that 128 pages are printed on a single sheet—64 pages on one side and 64 on the other. The process of making the press ready—placing the plates on the flat bed of the press, lining them up so that the margins will be equal, adjusting the pressure of the ink

A "form" of 64 plates or pages, in place on press, is given a last-minute check.

In photo on the opposite page the cylinder, wrapped by a sheet of paper, has just passed over the inked plates. The sheet is now printed on one side.

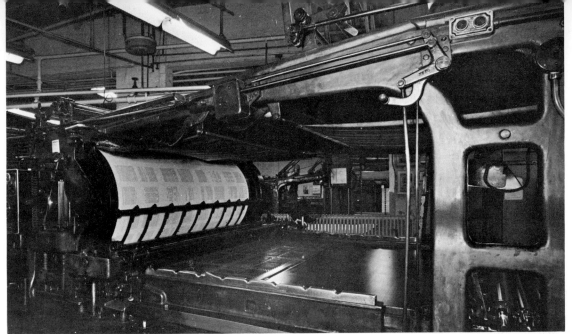

rollers so that the printing is not too light or dark—is a lengthy procedure lasting three to six hours, and must be carefully done by an expert pressman.

Once the make-ready is completed, the presses roll. The paper to be printed is stacked in a special rack in one end of the press. Metal arms with suction cups or grippers lift a sheet from the stack, insert it onto a cylinder around which the sheet is wrapped. This huge cylinder rolls over the inked plates on the bed of the press, and the sheet emerges at the far end freshly printed on one side. When all sheets have been so printed, new plates are inserted in the press, and the sheets are turned over to be run through the press again to print the "back-up" or reverse side. This process is repeated until all pages are completed. Thus, by the process described above, a book of 512 pages would require four sheets of paper, each put through the press two times, for a total of eight runs.

Other presses print both sides of a sheet on the same run of that sheet through the press. On still others the plates are curved and placed on cylinders. A roll of paper, sometimes six feet wide, is placed at one end of the machine and carefully threaded between the rollers. Such a press, called a "rotary," is designed so that one set of plates will print one side of the sheet while plates on a second roller will print the second side. The continuous roll of paper emerges from the far end of the press and is frequently cut into the correct sections as it emerges.

A view of a flatbed press, showing unprinted sheets starting at the right and emerging, printed, onto the delivery platform.

Plates to be used on rotary presses must be curved to fit onto a cylinder.

This large press cuts the roll of paper, seen at far right, into sheets, prints them from curved plates, and delivers sheets onto platform at the left.

LITHOGRAPHIC OR PHOTO-OFFSET NEGATIVES ARE MADE

So far, one type of plate and one type of press have been described. Another method commonly used today to print books is known as "lithography," often called "photo-offset printing." The first step in producing lithographic or photo-offset plates is to obtain from the type that has been set a clean, clear type proof—much clearer than the rough proofs pulled to check for errors. Such clean proofs are carefully made on special proving presses and on special paper. These are called "reproduction proofs."

Next, these proofs are turned over to the camera department of a lithographic plate making company. An expert photographer using a large camera, similar in size to that on page 23, makes negatives of the reproduction proofs. He also makes negatives of the photographs or drawings for the book, just as they are photographed for the engravings used in letterpress printing. From this point on, the two methods of printing are entirely different. When all the photographs, drawings, and reproduction proofs of a book have been photographed, the resulting negatives are sent to the lithographer's "stripping room." Those who work in this section of the plant cut page-size holes in large sheets of special paper, called "goldenrod," and fasten the negatives over these holes with Scotch tape. A sheet of this paper with all the negatives in place is called a "flat." Such flats are frequently large enough to include as many as 64 pages of a book.

The metal slugs of type used to print the reproduction proofs may now be thrown back into the pot of the typesetting machine and melted. They are of no further use, since photo-offset printing does not use type, but rather photographic negatives of type. Indeed, material that comes from a regular typewriter can be photographed just as readily as type-set material. It will not be as clean and sharp, however, as set type.

In the stripping room negatives of individual pictures and blocks of type are taped onto large "flats," from which a single lithographic plate is made.

Courtesy of Rae Lithographers

OFFSET PLATES ARE ETCHED

After the flats for an offset book have been made in the stripping room, they are sent to the offset plate department. Plate making for offset printing is quite different from that for letterpress printing. In the letterpress method, the halftone or line image is etched deeply in an acid bath, but in offset the plates are etched only a few thousandths of an inch.

The large, thin sheets of aluminum or zinc to be used for offset plates are thoroughly cleaned by placing them in an acid solution for a few seconds. The acid is then washed away with running water, and the plates are coated with a chemical that is sensitive to light. This chemical is poured on the plate as it is spun rapidly in a whirling machine. The spinning action causes the chemical to spread evenly over the entire surface of the metal plate.

When a plate has been coated with chemical and dried, a flat of the negatives is placed over it. The plate maker then places the metal plate and negatives in a vacuum frame to hold the flat tightly against the plate, and switches on a bright light. The light shines through the clear sections of the negatives in the flat to expose the chemical on the plate.

Carefully separating the flat from the plate, the plate maker uses a soft cloth or a sponge to smear developing acid over the exposed plate. As he applies the acid, printed words and photographs or drawings start to appear just as they will appear in the book. When all of the exposed sections are clear and black, the engraver floods the printing plate with water. The developing ink washes away from the sections that will be white in the book, but remains on the parts that will print.

Smearing developing ink over the plate etched from the flat of negatives, the lithographer carefully watches the copy to be printed emerge.

Courtesy of Rae Lithographers

PRINTING BY OFFSET

In letterpress printing generally there is one plate for each page. Thus, to prepare a press for one "form" or to print one side of a sheet of paper, as many as 64 plates must be carefully locked into position before printing. Photo-offset plates being large sheets of thin metal, again often with 64 pages to a sheet, it is necessary only to position a single metal sheet to ready the press. This huge metal sheet is wrapped around the large cylinder of the photo-offset press.

Unlike the letterpress method of printing, the offset press does not print directly from the engraved plate to paper. Photo-offset printing is based on the fact that water and grease will not mix. The printing plate on its cylinder first revolves against a roller dampened with water which wets areas of the plate that were not etched by the greasy developing ink. In the next revolution of the cylinder, ink is applied to the printing areas of the plate. The third revolution transfers the inked image to a rubber blanket wrapped around another roller. This cylinder of rubber is much softer than paper and will not damage the plate. The cylinder with the rubber blanket next rolls against the paper and transfers or "offsets" the ink to the paper.

After all sheets have been printed on one side, the printing plate is removed, a new one put in its place, and the sheets run through the press a second time to print the reverse side. As in the letterpress method, some offset presses can print both sides of the sheet in one run through the machine. Some presses will also print on a roll of paper, which is cut apart as it emerges from the press.

Instead of one plate the press on the left uses two, each printing a different ink on the sheet going through it.

Courtesy of Rae Lithographers

A small photo-offset press, showing two of the many cylinders necessary to transfer the image on the plate to paper.

BOOK JACKETS ARE DESIGNED

Almost every book in a bookstore or library has a paper wrapper or "jacket" around it, often a colorful one intended to catch your eye.

Much effort and time are spent by the publisher to produce this jacket. Not only must it be attractive, but it must tell quickly what kind of book it is—a dog story would perhaps have a drawing of a boy with his dog; a book about the making of books might have a photograph of a binding machine on it.

Publishers rely on artists and designers to work out the jackets. The art director of a publishing house will work at length with an artist, going over ideas for illustrations or the use of photographs, deciding the colors to be used in printing the jacket and the size and kind of type for the title, author's name, and description of the book. Then the artist carefully prepares the needed art work, perhaps making a special drawing, perhaps using a photograph and carefully lettering the necessary words.

When the art work and design are completed and approved, the art director can proceed to have the necessary plates made and to arrange for the printing of the jacket.

Meanwhile, the editorial and promotion departments are working together to produce the material that appears on the jacket "flaps" which fold into the book. This will include a description of the book's contents, perhaps a brief biographical sketch of the author, and related information. Such material must be carefully written, then set into type, and proofs thoroughly checked. Finally, the type joins the plates of the jacket art work.

The artist for the jacket of this book carefully works out the design, determining the kind and location of the lettering, and prepares necessary layouts.

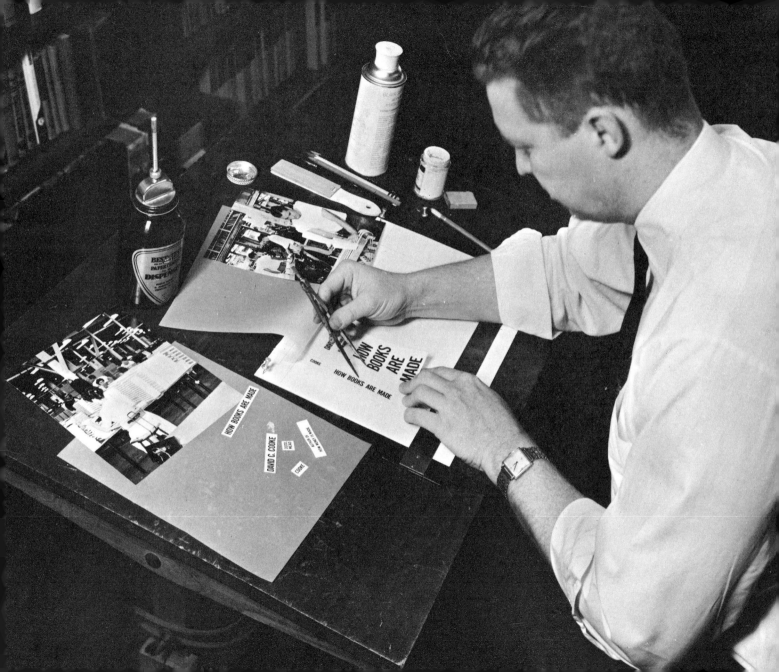

JACKET PLATES ARE ENGRAVED

It is not too difficult to understand how type or drawings or photographs are reproduced in black on paper. Use black ink and it prints black. If a solid red or green is needed, simply ink the press in the color desired and print. But how can a beautiful photograph in many colors, of a lovely sunset for example, be reproduced on paper so that it appears with all its hues just as in the original?

Since many jackets have colorful illustrations or photographs on them, here is a good place to describe how color is reproduced in printing. Whether a single jacket or a whole book is printed in color, the methods to produce these are the same.

One method, which is very commonly used, is known as "four-color process." The principle of this process is that any color is composed of the three primary colors—red, blue, and yellow. The photo-engraver who is to reproduce a photograph in full color must take four separate pictures with his camera. First he will place between the illustration he is photographing and his camera a special filter with the thousands of dots described on page 25. When the camera takes the picture through an orange filter, only those colors which have blues in them are exposed on the camera's negative. To be sure, some colors have more blue than others, but the camera carefully filters the dark blues as well as the light blues. Then the engraver uses a green filter which lets through the reds; next a violet filter for the yellows. Finally, since even the best camera can make errors, he uses a special filter for the blacks. Theoretically, this last special filter should not be necessary, because black is a true combination of the three other colors. However, this last photograph through the special filter will ensure the engraver of getting anything that the other filters may have missed.

Each of the four plates, being inspected in photo on opposite page, is used in sequence to print one picture in full color.

Courtesy of Sterling-Regal Engraving Company, Inc.

From the four films the engraver produces plates as previously described, one for each color. These plates are then put on a press, one at a time, and the press is inked in succession with the four basic colors. Thus, if the yellow plate is first used, the press is inked with the yellow color and there is printed on paper an image in which appear the various values of the yellows in the original drawing or photograph. The press is then cleaned of that color, inked with blue, and the blue plate inserted. The paper on which the yellow image has been printed is run through the press again. This time the blues of the picture are printed over, and combined with, the yellows. The red plate follows, and finally the black, the press being re-inked for each color. The result is a reproduction of the original illustration, with all of the original colors in it. The printer must be very careful that the plates are printed one on top of the other precisely. Frequently you have seen pictures in color which are a little blurred when this over-printing is not exact. In press work such a fault is known as poor "register."

The type material on the jacket of a book, much of which may be in black, is printed when the black plate of the set of four-color process plates is run through the press.

Once all colors have been printed, frequently a thin coat of varnish is rolled over the jacket to protect the printing from smudging and to give it a glossy appearance.

This special proofing press for color work prints in turn each of the four colors as a sheet passes over the plates.

Courtesy of Sterling-Regal Engraving Company, Inc.

SHEETS ARE FOLDED

After a book has been printed and the ink on the paper thoroughly dried, the flat sheets, neatly piled on wooden racks or "skids," are delivered to the bindery. This may be a section of the plant where the printing was done or it may be a different factory in another city.

The first step in binding a book is to fold and refold the large printed sheets until the pages on that sheet are in the proper sequence. If you should take a sheet of typewriter paper, fold it in half, fold it in half again, four times in all, you would end up with a small pad of paper with 32 pages to it. Very roughly, this is what happens in a bindery to each printed sheet of the book. Such sheets are automatically fed into a large machine called a "folder." Metal arms quickly fold and refold until the sheet emerges looking like a small thin magazine. The folder is a precision machine that makes each fold exactly like the one before and can handle thousands of sheets every hour.

The folded sheets are called "signatures," each usually containing 16 or 32 pages. The book you are reading has four signatures of 16 pages each. Should you look at the top edge of a closed book, you will notice faint lines or very thin stripes, equally spaced, running lengthwise along the top. Each line is the start or end of a signature.

The size of each signature is slightly larger than the pages of the finished book will be, and most of the pages in this signature are uncut at the edges. Later a thin strip of paper will be trimmed from the top, front, and bottom edge so that the pages become unattached and even.

In large photo on opposite page the pressman lifts a printed sheet which will be folded and refolded into a "signature" of pages the size he holds in his right hand. In upper right photo flat sheets are fed into a folding machine, to emerge as signatures, seen in the trays of lower right picture.

Courtesy of Vail-Ballou Press, Inc.

Courtesy of Kingsport Press, Inc.

SIGNATURES ARE GATHERED

When all sheets have been folded, the signatures that eventually become the first and last ones of the book are taken aside for a special operation. To the first page of the first signature and to the last page of the final signature is pasted a heavy folded sheet of paper, called an endpaper. This endpaper may previously have been printed with a design or may be plain white. These endsheets play an important part in the book binding at a stage to be described later.

Once the endpapers have been applied, all the signatures are transferred to another part of the bindery for "gathering." Gathering consists of collecting the various signatures of the book into their proper sequence and is done by machine, a large

Gathering machines automatically collect in sequence the signatures of each book.

complex one. Stacks of each signature are placed at various stations along one side of this machine. There may be sixteen such stations if the book is to have 512 pages of sixteen 32-page signatures. A mechanical arm picks the first signature of the book from its station and drops it on a moving platform. As this signature comes to each station, new signatures are automatically added until the last signature has been included.

As the gathered signatures come to the end of the machine, an inspector picks up each pile, one at a time, and flips through it to be sure that only one signature has been added at each station.

Courtesy of Kingsport Press, Inc.

The arms of a gathering machine select in the correct order the signatures of a book.

49

GATHERED SIGNATURES ARE SEWN

Since the several separately printed signatures or groups of pages which make up one book are loose, the next step is to fasten these together. This is done in the same way the pieces of cloth in a suit or a dress are fastened—by sewing.

There are several sewing methods. Very thin books of 16 or 32 pages can simply be wire-stitched along the inside edge. Another method for the thin book is to "side sew" it, running the signatures through a machine that stitches them together with a heavy

Each signature in its proper order is fed into a special sewing machine which stitches one to the next.

Courtesy of Vail-Ballou Press, Inc.

thread along the inside edge. Books so sewn do not lie open easily, but they are extremely sturdy. Generally the signatures of books more than a half-inch thick are sewn together on a "Smyth" machine, which runs threads into the very middle of each signature and carefully nips the very inside edge of that signature to hold one to the other. If you carefully open such a book in the center of a signature, you will see the holding thread.

Still another method of holding signatures together requires no sewing at all, but a very special glue. Here the inside edges of the signatures are first trimmed clean. Next a coat of special glue is applied to this edge, glue which slightly permeates the pages of the book, holding one page to the other. When this glue dries, the pages are held fast even when pulled individually. Such a method of gluing is called "perfect binding."

Courtesy of Kingsport Press, Inc.

Many sewing machine operators and inspectors of sewn signatures are necessary to produce one edition of a book.

SEWN SHEETS ARE SMASHED, TRIMMED, GLUED AND ROUNDED

The next step in binding is to "smash" the sewn sheets to press out excess air and to compress pages for tight binding. This is done by a machine that tightly squeezes the sheets. Signatures so smashed then have their edges trimmed off, accomplished by placing them into a cutting machine that drops a huge heavy, knifelike blade onto the three unsewn edges, trimming off about ⅛ inch of paper and leaving these edges clean and smooth. All pages are thus separated.

Most books, especially thick ones, are slightly rounded along the sewn edge or "spine." Such rounding also means that the front edge is concave or bowed in. This

"Smashing" sewn sheets. Note thickness of one book before and after smashing.

Courtesy of Kingsport Press, Inc.

Edges of sewn signatures are trimmed smooth in a cutting machine equipped with heavy, razor-sharp blades.

Courtesy of Vail-Ballou Press, Inc.

Courtesy of Kingsport Press, Inc.

The backs or "spines" of trimmed signatures are rounded by a rocking metal plate.

Courtesy of Vail-Ballou Press, Inc.

Strips of special cloth are automatically glued to the spines, and signatures emerge to receive their covers.

concave edge makes for better binding and easier reading. The making of the rounded spine is the next step in binding and is done by a machine that holds the signatures firmly together as a rounded hard metal plate is rocked against the spine.

The signatures then are given reinforcement along the spine by being sent through a machine that applies glue there, adds a strip of special cloth about 2 inches wider than the thickness of the book and a final strip of reinforcement paper.

While each step described above can be done on separate machines, special machines have been developed that do these steps in one continuous operation.

COVERS ARE MADE

While the sheets are being folded, gathered, and sewn, in another department of the bindery the heavy outside cover is being made separately. The cover or "case" of a book consists of a durable piece of heavy cardboard covered, usually, with cloth, though paper, leather, and other materials are used. Two pieces of cardboard are needed for each book, one for the front and the other for the back. These are cut by

Sheets of special cardboard are cut to the right size to fit the book.

Courtesy of Kingsport Press, Inc.

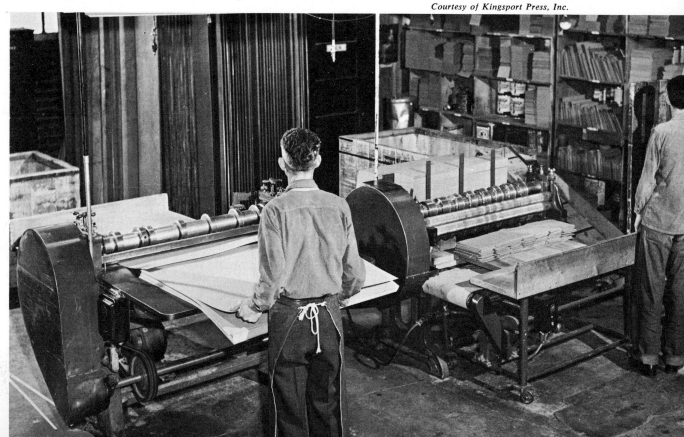

machine from sheets to a size slightly larger than the page of the book, to give a slight overhang or "lip" that will protect the paper edges.

On another machine pieces of the cloth or of the material to cover the boards are being cut from large rolls to the correct size. Occasionally the cloth is run through a press and a picture or design printed on it.

The machine below applies glue to the continuous roll of cloth, automatically feeds the boards and spine reinforcement strip onto the cloth, cuts each cover apart, and turns the overlapping cloth edges onto the boards.

Courtesy of Vail-Ballou Press, Inc.

The cut board and the cloth are next fed into a machine which carefully applies glue to the inner side of the cloth, positions the cardboard on the cloth, inserts a heavy strip of paper where the spine of the book will be located, and finally turns over the edges of the cloth onto the board. The finished cover is then fed between heavy metal rollers to squeeze the glue tight and to eliminate air bubbles.

If the cloth of the cover has not been previously printed, the finished cover must then be stamped on the spine and often on the front with the book's title, the author's name, and the publisher's imprint. To do this a brass plate or "die" must be made with the names in raised type on it, similar in appearance to the type on a printing plate, but in deeper relief. A simple kind of printing press, known as the stamping press, is employed to transfer the lettering of the die onto a cover. The die is inked with the desired color and then pressed hard against the cover, or a ribbon of metallic foil, such as gold or silver, is inserted between the die and the cover, then the two are pressed together. The result in either case is a clean impression on the cover of the names and words needed.

Courtesy of Kingsport Press, Inc.

Finished covers are inspected and stacked, ready for stamping.

At right covers are stamped in a special press with the book's title, author's name and appropriate decoration.

Courtesy of Vail-Ballou Press, Inc.

BOOKS ARE CASED IN

The final step in book binding is to combine the case with the sewn and trimmed sheets. This last operation is called "casing in."

Remember that earlier in the binding operation a folded sheet of heavy paper (end-paper) had been glued to the first page of the first signature and to the last page of the last signature. Later (page 53) a strip of cloth and one of paper had been glued to the spine or sewn edge of the signatures. These pieces will hold the cover to the sewn sheets.

The casing-in machine applies a special paste to the outer sides of the endpapers

A section of a "casing-in" machine, showing sewn sheets with spine cloth strip entering in lower part of photo and stacked covers in center pile ready to drop onto sheets.

Courtesy of Vail-Ballou Press, Inc.

and to the overlapping spine cloth strip. The cover is then wrapped around the sheets and squeezed very tightly. Some casing-in machines apply heat with the squeeze and in a few minutes books are completed. Other books are kept under pressure without heat for a day before being completed.

The sewn sheets have just joined their cover within the casing-in machine. The white paste has been applied automatically to the outside of the endsheets which are about to be pressed against the cover.

Courtesy of Vail-Ballou Press, Inc.

BOOKS ARE JACKETED, INSPECTED AND PACKED

The finished books are now ready to have the jackets placed on them. When many copies of one title are involved, the jacketing is done by machine. If the edition is small, trained men and women quickly do it by hand, at a rate of 500 books per person an hour.

Finally, the book is given a last inspection. A bindery inspector quickly riffles through each copy, discarding those books which are imperfectly bound—lacking a signature, or having upside-down covers, torn sheets, et cetera. Such imperfect books can often be repaired.

Then the books are stacked on wooden platforms or skids, as many as 500 copies to a skid, or packed into large cardboard boxes holding 30 or 40 copies. Now these are ready for the publisher's instructions.

Courtesy of Kingsport Press, Inc.

(Opposite) The last step in book making is the placing of printed jackets around the bound books and the inspecting of each copy for defects.

(Right) Finished books are packed into cartons and stored, ready for shipment.

A BOOK IS PUBLISHED

While the production department in the book-publishing company has been busy supervising the book's manufacture, other departments of that company have been active on behalf of the book. Salesmen have been out contacting book stores, libraries, schools, to take orders for the book. The advertising and promotion departments have been preparing newspaper ads, arranging window displays, and possibly organizing an autographing party for the author.

Once finished books are ready, advance copies are sent to reviewers, to bookstore managers, to librarians and to others who might influence the sale of the book.

Finally comes the book's official birthday, its publication date, generally a month after its manufacture has been completed. By the publication date, books have been received in stores all over the country, reviewers have prepared their columns, and advertisements have been readied.

Publication date may be years after the author first had an idea for the book; it may be months after the manuscript was first turned over to the production department. This publication date is all-important to the hundreds of people who had a hand in creating and making the book—the author, the editors, designers, compositors, pressmen, binders, and many others—for this is the time that you, the person for whom the book was made, first may read it and judge it.

INDEX